Love Continuum

Part I

By Aria Knox

Printed in the United States of America

Cover design by Elaina Lee.
Page layout by FreedomInk Publishing.
Initial edit by FreedomInk Publishing.
Final proof by Ja'Maela Byrd &
Katandra Jackson Nunnally.

First Printing, 2015

ISBN 978-0-9861001-4-7

FreedomInk Publishing
P O Box 1093
Reidsville, Georgia 30453

www.freedomink365.com

1. Poetry: Love
2. Poetry: Women Authors
3. Poetry: General

Acknowledgements

My goodness, I cannot believe that I've finally reached the point where I can say that I've written a book. This has been my passion for many years and the project itself is near and dear to my heart because I'm giving everyone a glimpse of my innermost self.

I want to first thank my Lord and Savior for blessing me with the ability to open my heart and pen this compilation of personal expressions. I have spent many years trying to find my voice and faith in God was the only safe haven.

A special thank you goes to my parents, you guys are so awesome! Your constant love and support has made me the woman and writer that I have become and I could never thank you enough for all that you sacrificed for me. Thank you for being there for me in every way possible and allowing me the room to grow. Next I must shout out my siblings, each and every one of you have both inspired and influenced me to be a better me and for that I'm forever grateful. I love you all from the bottom of my heart.

This book is centered on love so it's only fitting to thank the loves of my life, past and present. I have learned so much from the experiences that I've shared with you and for that I thank you. To my crazy friends, ya'll know I love ya'll! Thank you for the late night phone calls, text messages, girls' night out, everything. Thank you for listening and supporting my dream. Last but certainly not least I want to acknowledge my daughter. My greatest accomplishment is being your mother and it's a blessing to know that God loved me enough to send you.

May you all enjoy the journey in the
Love Continuum.
-Aria Knox

Dedication

To all lovers, the feeling is nothing short of extraordinary.

Love Continuum

Part I

By Aria Knox

Part I

...Love entered and made me whole.

Perfectly Flawed

Eyes that tell the story of a thousand lies
Paints the picture of a memory
and our lives.
Lips that speak the words
Hollow unto my ears
Be the depth of the soul that lives within.
Beauty as it seems
Conjure the spirit of thyself
In the midst of uncertainty,
Hands that touch beyond the heart
In the space where God dwells.
Be that as it may
Goosebumps down the spines of the spineless
As not to uncover truths.
We are frauds
Perfectly flawed, flawed perfectly.
The breeze infused with juniper blanket our tears and
evoke fears
Joy and pain are one and the same
As love slips from your lips
The decadent fruit
I divulge in the charm
Of a mystical being such as yourself
You arise from the flames
Phoenix you are
Perfectly flawed, flawed perfectly
And kisses, sweet kisses seal the fate
Of yesterdays and tomorrows.

A Beautiful Moment

Like a photo cast in black and white,
He is timeless.
A picturesque vision of sheer perfection,
Could anyone be so rare?
It seems we have visited this place before,
Tread along the waters, grazed the shore
But my eyes have never seen anything more beautiful.

It's subtle even,
The curve of his lips,
How they form that unique bow.
Ripened for the intensity of my kiss
On the stage of a one-man show.
To be his words, to know what he knows,
Rolling smoothly over his tongue.
I would savor his flavor, chocolate and mint.

He's so abstract and
I'm caught in the winding ribbon of his voice
As deep pools of mocha
marry amber flecks of gold
And birth the most beautiful eyes to ever appear on a
face so perfect.
I lose myself under the fan of his lashes
and allow my cheeks to catch his tears
while I kiss away the bitterness of his fears.

When he reads I strain my eyes to see what he sees,
View life from his lenses,

Love him as he cleanses my soul.
I fathom he knows that he is the object of my
intense scrutiny
For little me studies each and every line and trace on
his glorious face.
My head upon his chest,
The beating drum,
his heart the constant hum.
A rhythm permeating through me
so I begin to slowly move my feet, syncopated, the
movement is easy.
I dance on white clouds as he leads the song of the
legends
Playing smooth jazz in a round.
Encased in his embrace I could embed myself within
his heat,
Become one mind, one body,
one transparent soul.
Exist in gaiety, understand its toll.
I am transfixed in this moment
And he is poised and enchanting.

The planes of his frame are the membrane that keep
my nucleus in place.
Strong hands that splay at the small of my back,
Be the driving force of the internal
love's race.
Who could imagine a feeling so earthy?
Like he was taken from the rib of an oak
I dare not close my eyes
For fear that this vision will fade behind closed lids.

So I stare at what God created... Man.
I'll take you straight, no juice with my gin
No prayer for my sin
You are the fix for my heart broken, a beautiful
moment.

Organically United

When an eclipse occurs
the sun kisses the moon
Perfect is the union...
Reminiscent of my feelings for you.
When love is the flowers in bloom
And the sky cries springing life forth from earth
Deeply within one another
we are consumed.
Onyx, midnight eyes I stare into
just like glass prisms
You have captured me
And I am victim in your love prison.
Perfection is the essence of your being
And I am innately embedded
within your soul
The vision of a perfect dream.

Tangled

You are a phrase repeated constantly
A conundrum
That can't be solved,
Could I be the center of your universe?
Love you near and far?
You're masterfully created
and my fingertips
are the brushes that love to stroke the canvas
that is your skin.
I'll allow my limbs to be tangled
Effortlessly taken by you.

Natural Rhythm and Blues

I remember when rhythm and blues would make my
heart pulsate
Then we would catch the break
And rock steady to the groove
The groove that was you... My music.
Defining my existence,
reminiscent of a time when the bass hit
and we were the perfect fit... My muse.
My palms read everything
I wish my eyes would see
To learn from the past
Is to know the new me
But you're a new note
New sound
New rhyme...

Complex Souls

My eyes don't shed tears
Stained face, my washed away fears
Love slipped from your hands like sand
Emotions erupt from within me
Remembering our beginning...
Cherished lover, I've loved no other
Still you're fixated to keep us asunder.
I wryly smile, my guard keeps me
from screaming
You find pleasure in it, beaming
Mocking my diligence,
Relevance in this game
where you make the rules
Carefully I hold your love
like precious jewels
And I only coexist in a world where you
are domineering
Arbitrarily designed my soul
With complex engineering.

6:24 a.m.

I walk alone in my mind,
My heart itself is a lie.
Once captured loves splendor
And now my surrender
Fallen mistakenly, awaken me.

The slumber deep and pure
For all that I had was yours
Upon eyes that shone brightly
by the sun's rays
Reminiscing of our past and better days.
Like a statue I am frozen in time,
Searching my mind for the words to formulate the
sentence
I begin my repentance
And fluidly these words flow from me
As I am drained of my gifts
Depleted of my heart's joy
And it's you that I miss.

Understand my soul,
but you jeopardize the whole
Picture that we've painted
And the love that we have created.
Like an angel with clipped wings
you fell from the heavens
Let's attribute our meeting to chance
Or luck, like rolling sevens
Toxic describes what we are to one another

But as there is breath in me
I'll only need you, lover.
So I tread through the night
in search of you,
Desperate to have your figure in view.

If your heart should stop
then you could have mine
Trying to find semblance in this place
at this time.
Where we hide from the world
in our cocoon
In each other's arms staring at the moon.
As the sounds of the city lulls us to sleep
I am more invested in you and far too deep.
I long to live where your heart rests
So I hold you closely
with my head on your chest.
Love so strong, powerful and ours
I place sweet kisses on your lips
the delicate flower.
As dawn breaks and the day begins
I remember that once you were my friend.
Upon realizing your
disappearing act
once more
My heart decides to even the score.

Go

I fathom my heart sinking to my stomach
Is pleasurable to you
The control it takes to keep
my mind in place
Along the edge of nonexistence in the humane race.
Are you contrite at all?
Do you feel the fear of disappointment?
There's a never ending beading of sweat
That cascades along my face masking tears
Has my love always been like this?

I approach you in fear and trepidation
Trying to catch a glimpse of a mood
less melancholy.
Watching the clock as my
blood pressure rises
With each moment that passes
I am further a lost soul
Longing for freedom but my heart
won't let me go
But through the fire
There is comfort here.

Cold War

He was cold, his chill
Broke the seal of my heart
Barricaded by storm doors
Knocked down at start
But I follow his memory
As though it were my life's blood.
My heart is covered and cloaked with unfamiliar
garments
Its essence is disguised
By the dream of what once was
And never again.

Finding The Lost

When the merriment of life's festivities cease
My soul cries for refuge from the storm that has
descended
Forcing cries and crushing dreams.
What once was is now shattered fragments
of a being mended.
With open arms I catch the flame,
And your tongue wags blades
piercing my body with every word spoken.

Calloused hands on my skin
I cringe at how I've given so much
Holding my thoughts for safe keeping,
dying inside I'm broken
Stolen moments of past times and slick lines
I fell victim to the beast.
Tears no longer care to fall and words no longer form
Our selfishness has me bursting at the seams
Nonexistent, reminiscent of a time too familiar
I race through the abyss, hoping to find her.

Vertebrae

Severed in places
Unable to repair
Whole feelings made half
By one delicate stare.
If I could stretch, I might be able to stand
Straighten my neck,
And feel my hands.
Inhaling deeply to exhale on a sigh
Tilting my head upward
To look towards the sky
Up there I'd find the answers that I seek
Uncovered, so beautifully
Up there I'd retreat.
My angles are complex
And vivid is the sight
When feeling isn't real anymore
And falling is my plight.

Air

In the open air we breathe...
In something beautiful we believe.
Lights that flash behind my minds' eye
At last I've found my soulmate.
Starving for wisdom you have filled my plate,
Quenched my thirst.
Let weeping willows pillow us
As we rest in the arms of the universe.
When midnights lurked
And daylights hurt
You gave me insight and I found solitude in you.
When life left me black and blue
As my eyes burned and tears welled
I studied and learned you well.
My heart ached to feel and its beats raced
That I might fall into your embrace.

I'm enthralled with the motion of your lips
as you speak.
In your eyes the future I steal a peek.
Anticipating tomorrow, remembering yesterday,
Reveling in today.
Wildflowers in misty blue,
I'm chronically moved by you.
You singe my skin at the onset of touch
A sweet and serene metaphysical rush.

Gray Matter

A paraplegic by love
I conquer its fury
A microscopic stain so gray.
Yellow and pinkish hues
Covering the blues,
Sensory nerves tangled in a web of impulses ignited.
My myelinated axons burst with the electric charge
you stimulate.
Gray matter...
Sensory perception acutely in tune with you,
Vehemently, you I assimilate.

Goodnight Red Skies

If I were free…
I would simply be, understand that time is a continuum
Which leaves no space for doubt.
Underneath shady willows
My surrender hovers above.
Dark clouds of misguided hope
Are thrown away love songs
And recycled bitterness.

I would uncage the beast that lives within,
Unlock the fury that lies dormant
Hold on to unconscious thought
For matter is elemental.
Reserve my anticipation for a time when
We are but molecular bonds entwined by love
But we don't see it,
Nor do we believe it.

We dance in the flames
Careful not to burn
For the scorching of our indiscretions
are our lessons learned
But I feel,
For a moment I feel again.
And where the corridor to my heart was blocked
By red skies and cold nights
The ice in my eyes cracked with one kiss goodnight.

Rhapsody In You

There is a feeling that takes over,
A rush of emotions so beautifully kept
That my mind gets lost in the play of things.
There is a rhythm that moves my feet,
Vibrating gift so benevolent that my blood pulsates to
the chords on your orchestrated spine.

Upon the first touch,
A sting left by the imprint of your fingertips burn still.
Soul stirring kisses that linger
Unwrapping secrets hidden within.
Eyes like glass orbs be the crystal ball
Giving insight to the future.
I am engrossed in the moment.
You cloak me with your embrace
One could not fathom the warmth found there.
For in that instant we are one mind,
one soul, one thought.

Surely it is possible to feel the chill of anticipation and
heat of longing all at once,
To fall deeper into the abyss,
yet fly high above the clouds.
You inexcusably defy the laws of physics
For there is no science to describe you.
No words to truly captivate all that is...you.
You're a feeling, an emotion, presence,
a beam of sunshine on a warm summer day.

How the ocean blue moves fluidly in
Conjunction with the wind,
That calm is what I feel when you are near me.
I am so entwined in you that I would risk my life
in solitude
For the chance to simply look at you.
Certainly we are uninhibited
For you awaken my inner being.
The person that the world sees is only a fraction of
who you've made me.
I am alive and you are beautiful.

Summer Mornings

I watch the sun rise above the horizon,
Warms my soul to see you there.
I hear the birds outside my window
Their proverbial love song stays with me.

I forget my own name until you speak it,
Compose a masterpiece and you teach it.
I am but a fairytale trapped in a nightmare,
Yet you saved the day.
Gently and purely,
you blow me away.

In Dreams

A beautiful dream,
you happened quite the same
I wished for it and you called out my name.
I followed your voice into the deep dark night
Traveling until I stumbled
upon a love that felt right.
I did not question its validity or candor
Because I wanted you more thereafter.
So in my drunkenness intoxicated by you,
I stepped into the light to get a clearer view.
A simple glance at the one
who stole my heart that day,
A love that remains the one that got away.

Nostalgia

Oh sand beneath my toes.
Where she's going? Nobody knows.
Oh sweet tea and childlike dreams.
Skipping rocks in parks and streams.
Nostalgic moments,
in her memory bank they stay...
Coins on the sidewalk meant good luck.
Holding hands when lightning struck.
They recite rhymes under moonlit skies.
Arranging flowers in her mind.
She fell victim to the wind,
her ending displayed before it began.
Shattered, bruised and battered.
The allure of the fast life,
is the way to pass time.
But her heart, precious jewel...
Infuses new days with old school.
Now and laters were confections.
A way to soothe her imperfections.
What once was long walks or summer strolls,
are now hard lines on a delicate face
marking life's toll.
But she's exquisite.
Mind before body is her prerequisite.
A penny for her thoughts,
like candy in corner stores.
When she dreams of days wanting more.

The World On Her Hips

The exterior exploits the beauty
resonating from within
From the finest follicle of perfectly coiffed hair
To the sweetest kiss of giving lips
Nothing in this world compares to December...
Her fullness of life exudes love,
Carrying the weight of the world on rounded hips
And eyes that tell the story of one thousand memories
While tears of blood are the keepsakes
of her struggle and pain.
Her triumph is a smile that brings new life to the world
With a passion that grows imminently.

Shadows

They follow me,
Haunting my dreams and stealing my memories.
They run after me as I attempt to hide in desperation
To no avail, I fail.

I am a mockery, confused and desolate,
I can hear the footsteps as their speed increases
Matching the rhythm of my beating heart.
Continuously pounding, excessively racing,
They follow me still.

Figments of my imagination, the steps are my own
In the depths of darkness I see the light in the distance.
But I am unable to reach what I long to hold close,
Relative closeness they appear and fear begins to
show.
Palpitations and perspiration persist as I begin to
unravel,
Searching my mind for the security that escaped so
long ago.
There is none.

They follow me,
Haunting my dreams, stealing my memories,
Creating havoc on my soul.
I've been gone from home too long;
Jaded pictures in the dark, running from the start
But I cannot escape the shadows left in the dark.

Part II

...broken like shattered stained glass, my heart lost its zeal for life and my variant colors began to fade.

The Email

I emailed you...
Allowed my heart to do the talking
As my fingertips glided across the keys
Erect and upright, + positioned at 90 degrees,
I needed to focus...
Become one with these words
for I was hopeless.
When I began my intention was to confess,
Profess the bountiful love that I felt for you
But as my fingers stroked the keys
Making love to dreams
Deferred was the prior course of my letter
Took the wrong turn, journey, and knew better.
Somewhere along the way I lost my purpose
Genuinely searching for meaning
but only scratching the surface.
For you to open up to me
Was far too much to ask
So I bit my lip and settled being last.
Oh the sweet taste of my broken flesh
Was but a memory of your kiss more or less
We danced through life as though
the last song was played
I envisioned you and me
and prayed that you'd stay
Naïve I guess, I wanted to be seen
Understood, remembered, maybe it was greed.
I turned my cheek and rested in the shadows
Impressed by your essence now seems so shallow.

The Experience

Your visual is appealing but I'm drawn to the unseen.
I could be educated by your kisses,
Your spoken words of wisdom, is this
the definition of infatuation or is it something more?
Could I engage you literally?
Let's explore.
I'll be the pupil in your classroom
School me and soon
I'll graduate with the highest degree of loving you.
Truth emanates from your eyes
The comfort there is why
My heart bleeds your life's blood
Connected... We have accepted
The riches that life affords us.
Angel sent from the heavens
Thus making my existence a possibility.
Rhythm to my blues, notes on my staff
Masterpiece for me meant to last.
Does the earth shift when our eyes meet?
Is it the power of our souls connecting we...
Are moved.
Lover be my guide, lighthouse in the distance
may I come inside?
Be the breeze to my summertime
The beat to my rhyme
Your lips, sweet November
Their imprint I'll remember
I pursue you with diligence
As we partake in the experience.

Surface Tension

I put pen to paper,
Allowed the words freely to bleed onto the paper
Settled in the mindset that now would soon be later
Wondering how I should word this
Fascinated with ink,
One could suspect
I write on the brink of insanity
Past none, my thoughts to collect
Because flesh colored band aids don't hide the wounds
The blazing heat turned stagnant breeze
I'm caught in my mind's monsoon
Of the world what am I missing?
I long to release the surface tension.

In My Mind

Away from skin drenched in perfumed perspiration
I aspire to inspire,
Dream to dream dreams
That will soon come true.
Away from tunnel vision
With precision the decision is
Mine alone...
I escaped the chains of my mind.

Filled to capacity
I implode my innermost self
In desperation to be...
Explode with material wealth
Oh my slit wrists from the razor of your tongue.
You lick the wounds with alcoholic venom
Cleansing the burn with vodka and rum.
A systematic withdrawal the rise and fall
My hurt is your motivation.
As cries and laughter are a direct correlation
I escape the reigns of my own mind.

Wrapped in a warped sense of time
Lost in losing
Scolded for forgiving as emotions flair on our sleeves
Holding a heart laden with jealousy,
In your heart you will remember me.
Remember the smoothness of my kiss,

The soothe of my gift.
Remember the first and last
Present and past
Caged in my mind.

Undone

We were masked,
Caught in the moment of
Present, future and past.
I was gliding on the wood floors,
Toes grazing the surface
As the music transported my soul to a place
so unlike like cage that held me captive.

It was an afterthought,
You, the building blocks
Of a love that I found beautiful.
Sharing my secrets, I confided in you,
Played jury to our cause
But like every song has an ending, so did we.

Mmm the sweet melodic groove
Of my body against yours was too potent to let go
So I allowed myself to be consumed,
Moved and drawn to your familiarity.
Our syncopated rhythm was enough to seal our fate
With my arms outstretched I reached for you
Knowing nothing more classic could exist.

In this moment, in this place
Could a heart be more full?
Bursting at the seams
I release my cries of passion
For you to catch a glimpse of me.
Your music, the song, the reverb

Of your voice was the implant that renewed me,
You were my vision, my love,
My soul tie and heart's joy
Undone.

When Ink Dries

The sweetest pain I've ever known
is the intricacy of your calligraphy on my pages.
Each stroke of your pen tell a story
that only I belong in.
The design of these words so passionate and pure
Breathes life into my pages with every turn.
I wait patiently for you to choose your ink,
Black; the pain in your eyes,
Blue; the freedom in your sky,
Red; bold loving and true
I am captivated by you in every hue,
Longing to create something beautiful too.
Let us write a manuscript and caress the lines,
Let me be the paper that your pen strokes
Before the ink dries.

Kingdom

Against rain slicked pavement,
The steady hum my feet pound.
Rhythmic sound...
I crane my neck to see the sun,
For in the clouds is freedom
On earth or his Kingdom.

Borrowed Time

I breathe, solemnly swearing
To swear you off but my body craves your touch
Cross my heart and hope to lie...
Next to you
Raw, passion, borrowed time
Take my body, heart and mind
With your key, you've unlocked Pandora's box
But I still hold secrets, kept keepsakes
Like that time, in that place
Shhhh... We don't speak of it
But one day we will
And when we do,
Will our hearts match our diligence to fight?
The world is so black and white
While, we are more abstract
And with our unconventional way of thought
Grey areas are most prevalent.
You surrender only half
and I silently pray for the whole
But I know better...

Venom

In between the raindrops are sparks of light
Falling from the heavens
Brightening life
Do we see it? Do we feel it?
Or are we simply existing... Being bathed by its
Superficial wash.
I wish my tears were sweet
Because the salty flavor of my hurt
Burns my tongue when I speak your name.

Soul Tied

I bare my soul to you,
Whispering it sweetly over
The glistening sheen of your skin.
My heart beats in tandem of the rhythm of your breath
and I wade there.
And if the crisp breeze were to harden my bones,
make me brittle and break,
I would still ache to have you.
Through fire and ice, cooled and heated again
by desire I am renewed.
For loving something never meant anything until I
began loving you.
But my eyes leak like a fall rain, cold and
temperamental...
Wet earth cushions the blow
as I faint in love for only one... You.

And So We Play

The clarity of our connection is unflawed
Beautiful and pristine.
Under hooded eyes I see inside your heart
Longing to be in your dreams
When night falls and the stars shine bright
I envelope myself within your warmth
My desolate self becomes a lovely sight
Hungry to be, one, reborn
And so my heart is etched with desire
Written in hieroglyphics
Balm to the white hot fire
Your manhood is prolific
Insanely entranced by the words you speak
Gently perusing my mind
Is it my soul that you seek?
Cursed by my reality, I drink in your wine
And fluently speak unto you in my native tongue
While the rest of the world sleeps
We search high and low for love
In the cavern of my boxed heart you creep
Haughtily, stretching my arms to the sky
The vision of perfection lies before me
To read the meaning deep within your eyes
I play again our secret scene.

For Someone

Do you only exist in dreams and premonitions?
My mind ponders the thought often
Since my heart can feel your presence.
For that I am commissioned
To follow the halo of light in the distance.
So near yet so far
like the earth floating in the universe.
I'll reach for the end of time
to catch a glimpse of your smile.
Unscathed by the world's view... I'll love you first.
Your hues pull me in
Though my eyes have never seen anything quite like
Bright rays, a moth to a flame.
In no formalities did we engage
Undying love, my being can sense your aura.
What others may succumb is fairy tale chatter,
I know better, need more.

I bleed for you and my affirmations of
love languages cannot explain enough
My hearts' joy to have you there.
Run through the rain under a moonlit sky with me.
In each other's eyes may we get lost in the stare,
Or simply meet underneath a willow
as the sweet breeze makes it's way home again.

Conjure up a love song
and play my heart's strings until you are content,
And I'll rest my head upon your chest

and become one with the intrinsic beat of your soul
And then... Breathe in the scent of you and commit
your fragrance to memory.
Cavalier actions I possess in the present
As my thoughts escape to a time
when you were my everything.
I'll gladly give up my inhibitions
to taste the sugar on your lips,
Honey, be the farthest thing
from just a vision of perfection
And we'll glide in the clouds with undulating hips.

Engulfed in our rhythm, your composition relieves me
For you are spiritual,
connected through space and time.
A ceiling of glass cannot limit our love or minds,
But I've imagined you, warm and sweet
To counteract the salt from tears
as they fall from my cheeks.
Breathtakingly beautiful story untold then some...
Exist in a world where magic unfolds for someone.

Part III

...and then I awoke with a renewed sense of being.

Slowly

Hold my hand while we walk in the night
That I might stare at the stars through your eyes
Kiss me slowly, let me spin
On the axis of love
Stop my heart and start it again.
Rest your head on the bosom
Of a full heart
And take me away with your wings open wide.
Your light shines, beacon of my hope.
Slowly kiss my lips
Stain them with the strokes
Of your tongue as we meld fiercely in bliss.
Slowly move my hips
Pelvis to pelvis we coast
On clouds awaiting each other's gifts
Slowly touch my heart.

Love Is

Love is sound traveling at the speed of light.
A gentle rustle of autumn leaves against pavement
and the faint hush of a summer rain.
It is the scent of a magnolia tree
bloomed to perfection.
The feel of the brightest ray of sun
caressing one's face.

Love is truth and jazz music,
blues and spreading of the gospel.
It is prestige, regality, wealth and poverty all
encapsulated within one heart.
Love is a blessing and a deep regret,
patience and insanity, confusion and clarity.
It is a beat, a life changing rhythm,
an uninhibited dance, song sung in tune,
a melody written for two.
Love is a concerto and line, a portrait and rhyme,
Love is yours and mine.

Strings and Pearls

My heart rate quickened at first glance of him
underneath the glow of amber lights
I wanted to be close.
I took center stage and he played my notes as
my body moved in tandem with his melody.
He stroked the keys and I imagined that my spine
were the ebony and ivory play things
that his fingertips
so precisely grazed...
I couldn't have been imagining the looks
as unbridled passion loomed within his eyes.
He wanted to hear my song and I wanted to sing it loud
but we played coy and left that moment on the stage.
Habitually we would stare at one another
and find solitude in the mystery.
I imagined his voice,
a timbre strong enough to melt my icy heart.
His touch with just enough pressure to leave his
imprint on my life forever.
Let it be him, I prayed
that I might exist for him to coexist with me.
For I would adorn him with my love.

The Kiss

Bitten lips, vain and profane love making,
Humble beginnings turn to complex assertion.
Confident in how we feel at this moment,
Marking territory with passion marks
Providing evidence of the deed.

Yet somehow incredulous of this kiss,
Devouring and savoring the depth of this passion,
everlasting.
Dancing tongues, our tribal initiation
Sending messages of life through
nerve endings ignited.
Soft whispers, enchanting music invading our senses
In amazement butterflies take flight
as this kiss is deep, strong and ours.

Fallen hearts caught by heavens love,
Entranced by what is to come
and losing ourselves completely
giving all that we possess.
Sweat beading as this hunger unfolds,
Love is released in a sea of ecstasy.
Consequently, unchartered waters sway this passion
Weakening minds and paralyzingly dreams.

Sweet Satiety

Simple kisses, hits and misses at the small of my back,
The tip of my tongue is poisoned
by his alcoholic loving.
So hungover, this love gets stronger
And I struggle to escape the prison
of his sensuous touch.
Love surrenders,
sending tiny flutters through my heart
For I am lost and have forgotten all matter.
I scream out as our hearts beat in tandem,
This lovemaking is much more than
A random act of kindness, existence aflame.
He soothes me with his simple kisses
And I am satiated.

Perplexed

Emotions flood my mind with thoughts of you at times.
You see beyond tomorrows
and I am a permanent fixture in your yesterdays.
I wonder if I should revisit where you rest,
where we played.
You comprehend my not so secret innuendos,
But in life's play, you are a one-man show
If ever there were a time
for a woman to simply dream,
I could say I love you; and you would finally know.

Love Continuum

The potency of affection
Given by simple contact is reverent
in the bow to their feet
Every soul catching glance
A milestone of those memories passed
Playing scene by scene before them.
Love exists on singed skin,
Burned by the aftermath of their white flame.
Where imprints from fingertips are left as evidence
On balled fists,
Where blood rushes in a whirl and capillaries burst as
the pressure of this
incomprehensible love affair takes flight
In the night sky, above city lights, they fly...
As one heart leaps into the chest of the other
The moon casts its glow.
And upon midnight they rise, forever intrinsic.
He is suffocated by her radiance and desperately gasps
for a breath of she.
What is merely an explosion of hydrogen and oxygen,
A star is born and her light shines eminently.
As the time space continuum exists there is no room
for a diluted sense of being.
When the first sign of dawn peeks through the clouds,
The perpetual race begins
With stolen moments and wounds open
They adorn their disguises.
But should difference at all matter
When chasing love is the latter?

Dreaming In Song

I was stargazing underneath a cherry tree
When he sweetly sang his song to me.
I watched his lips as the melody outpoured
Lost in his moment, a soul tie was formed.

As if my beating heart could silence his tune
I searched for reverence under the light of the moon
But louder he became and harmoniously we swayed
Filling my heart's hollows, for me he sang.

Just A Thought

If my name were spoken from his lips
The venom of their connection to my heart
would cause me to die instantly.
Solemn it is in the night
As we lay here in manufactured bliss.
His sweat drips upon my chest and its burn
Forever a memory of how I want him to stop.
But I want him to stay.
Our kisses aren't blissful, they're foreign and cold,
Our embraces aren't wishful,
they're filled with empty promises
And and a life forged.
We cared too much for the thought of love
And missed it completely.
He wanted his mother and I needed a lover
So where do we go from here?
I'm too proud to admit that
my mistake was at the beginning.
He's to proud to let go,
he has to prove that he's winning.
But we're on the same side, the losing team,
and neither of us understands the pull.
I desire to be more than his after thought,
more than his embarrassment,
I long to be someone's muse.

Green with Envy

I don't like their flicker,
The gleam from the sun makes them more prominent.
Unmoved by their allure,
making a mockery of me I'm sure.
I left the door open and they walked in
Sat down their bag and unnervingly lifted their chin.
I should have viewed things from another angle
But who really expects to be invaded
by one of God's Angels?
Their mysterious web drew him closer
As he forgot that I existed for the chance to know her.
In the orbs where the light shines
He was lost in their twilight
So I hate green eyes...
It is them that I despise
Zeroing in on what is mine.
When vows were taken, we were sold on the dream
Faltering every year but I wanted to believe.
When my heart ached to understand his needs
He attached himself to anything that wasn't me.

I moved past the bitterness of hurt and despair
But there she was in the distance, flipping her hair.
I questioned myself wondering what were my faults?
For as much as I tried, my hopes and dreams were lost.
But in their moment he found all that he desired
And I became someone that I didn't know
as my soul burned through the fire.
With every word of love and care

I realized that I was not the one standing there
For she was his glory,
On his level, his speed.
While I was just the failure who carried his seed.
And in her orbs where the light shines
He was lost in her twilight
So I hate green eyes…
It is them that I despise
Zeroing in on what was mine.

Night Rain

I am one with the night as it rains,
Cold and mystic below the surface of blazing humidity.
I long to inhale your fragrance, woodsy and vanilla.
A candle ablaze before us,
Might I taste you and savor your
flavor on my tongue
As I bask in this moment.
You are familiar, and a gentle peace becomes me.
If memories are but dreams
that we intend to not forget
then I must be living in exactly that.
For this moment is precious and I care for it with the
warmth of my hands.
Rain drops fall like crystal candy on my lips
and I'll kiss you with with its sweetness.
It's always this way at night when it rains.

Conquered

I walk alone on a quest to freedom,
Believing that understandings are never missed.
For we're just a piece of a whole turning about face
As our lives intermingle in this
melting pot of foolishness.
Is there a time when faith loses its fullness and
relations miss the ship?
Are we on the road to redemption
or do we fall victim to sin?
It's a conundrum really,
a long drawn out expression of disappointment
As we express ourselves with selfishness.
In order to reconcile the fragmented hearts of past
loves, before I master thine, I'll conquer mine.

Mantra

Sometimes it follows me,
I wish that it would stop
but the continuous pace that I tread
Is no match for the swift movements of guilt.
Though years should grant me wisdom,
Instead I'm reduced to childlike actions
As I hide underneath the covers,
peeking to see if I'm truly as inconspicuous
As I would hope to be.

The fallacy of it all,
Basing our lives on untruths,
I was the jester sent to make you laugh.
But did you smile, did you ever smile?
To my expense I was haunted by your words
and moved by the idea
that I could somehow
fit into the world that you envisioned
...created.
There is a time when the cares of the world
no longer hold priority
And life is worth much more than someone else's
perception of it,
Or you... I've chosen to find me.

Author Biography

Aria Knox (Ja'Maela Byrd) was born and raised in Youngstown, Ohio and is the proud mother of a beautiful little girl. Writing has always been her passion and she discovered at a very young age that literature and expressing herself through words was not only therapeutic but innately a part of her being.

One who truly enjoys the arts, Aria is a singer/song writer and enjoys theater as well. Her poetry and personal expressions are often performed as songs. After a long term relationship with many ups and downs, life has propelled her to write down the accounts of her love life into a compilation of personal expressions that she has titled "Love Continuum", the authors first book. Her belief in love and its power is unyielding and the reason that Aria continues to write and create works with the general theme being centered on love.

FreedomInk Publishing
www.freedomink365.com

www.ingramcontent.com/pod-product-compliance
Lightning Source LLC
Chambersburg PA
CBHW032210040426

42449CB00005B/520